The Biblical Guide to Critical Thinking

Sharlyne Carla

Copyright © 2018 Sharlyne Carla

All rights reserved. No part of this book may be reproduced or transmitted in any form or by any means, electronically or mechanically, including photocopying, recording, or by an information storage and retrieval system without permission in writing from the author of this book.

Scripture quotations are taken from the King James Version of the Holy Bible unless otherwise indicated.

ISBN: 978-1-7326199-0-6

Published by:

P.O. Box 608297, Orlando, FL 32860
www.TakeUpThySword.com

Edited by:
Sigmarie Soto, Technical Writer & Editor
www.linkedin.com/in/sigmariesoto

Endorsements

"*The Biblical Guide to Critical Thinking* illuminates the essential bridge between business practices and Kingdom principles. Sharlyne Carla presents important, valuable practices based on relevant biblical foundation. She strategically addresses the value of subscribing to a clear formula for replicable decision making success. This book provides a concise informational guide anchored in the pivotal why at the center of the what and how of effective decision making." — **Roxanne Bellamy**, CEO, Bolder Spirit Productions, LLC

"When one considers biblical foundation, process, evaluating data and efficiency, this book collaborates to embrace each of the aforementioned principles and will promote better outcomes. Christian business professionals will benefit through the wisdom and value proposition of this text." — **Ken A. Bradshaw**, Financial Advisor, Prudential (President's Council)

"Looking for a simple guide to making a decision? Sharlyne has provided valuable insights to decision-making, while employing critical thinking skills all from a biblical perspective. The stories she cites, along with her own experiences, delivers much needed guidance when moving forward in life and business." — **Tarsha L. Campbell**, Entrepreneur & Certified Empowerment Coach

"POWERFUL and PROFOUND... This book is a must read indeed. Filled with wisdom that inspires, knowledge that empowers and an understanding that will provoke you to stop and think before you make your next decision... WOW! Sharlyne, job well done."
— **Tammy R. Green**, CEO of Gifted Designs by Tammy, Radio Talk Show Host, Author

"We are living in a world where our beliefs and actions are challenged daily. There is a need for an ethical and moral compass. Sharlyne Carla gives us one in this book." — **Dr. Gordana Pesakovic**, Business Program Chair, Herzing University

"As a Christian businesswoman, this is a must read. Through a simple step by step process, *The Biblical Guide to Critical Thinking* serves as a great reminder of how important it is to make good decisions in day to day business transactions and life in general. This is definitely a book worth adding to your collection!"
— **Mary Pitts**, Owner, Join Mary Pitts and Founder/CEO, Business Women Inspirational Network

"Having a child-like spirit can bring you to an openness that can lead you to greater awareness. But when that innocence becomes jaded and a deeper understanding is required, the importance of critical thinking becomes apparent. This book brings you that deeper understanding and a realization that Sharlyne Carla was touched to review. I highly recommend this book for your personal revelation, your family discussions and your reason for returning to reading."
— **Evangelist Angie BEE**, Award-winning Author, Media Producer, Promoter

"Various decisions concerning my companies have to be made daily. *The Biblical Guide to Critical Thinking* truly helped me to see decision making, using critical thinking, from a biblical perspective. The clarity I received from this book allowed me to understand that as a Christian business owner, my faith-based decisions should be in line with the perfect will of God. Sharlyne's insight is invaluable to those who have a Christ-centered business." — **Omega Mothersill**, Executive Director, Women Business Leaders and Entrepreneur Pageant

Introduction

The Biblical Guide to Critical Thinking provides a decision-making blueprint based on biblical principles that can be used in every aspect of life, especially in business affairs. The similarities between business-based critical thinking methods and stories found in the Bible are presented to give a balanced view of the most effective process for making good decisions. Critical thinking is explored by giving a comprehensive definition, habits and tools, and explaining how it should be utilized for proper decision-making. Biblical examples are illustrated throughout to clearly show the benefits of making good choices and the consequences of making bad choices. The information provided will enable the reader to make better decisions in order to facilitate the most favorable results.

Table of Contents

Critical Thinking Defined	8
Critical Thinking Habits	10
Critical Thinking in Decision-Making	13
Decision-Making Process	15
Benefits of Good Decisions	17
Decision-Making Outcomes	20
Decision-Making Experience	23
Conclusion	27
Bibliography	29
About the Author	30

Critical Thinking Defined

Critical thinking is defined comprehensively by the National Council for Excellence in Critical Thinking as "the intellectually disciplined process of actively and skillfully conceptualizing, applying, analyzing, synthesizing, and/or evaluating information gathered from, or generated by, observation, experience, reflection, reasoning, or communication, as a guide to belief and action" (Scriven and Paul, 1987). According to 1 Corinthians 2:16, a Believer should possess the wisdom of Jesus and therefore, be able to utilize a similar strategy for decision-making.

In the Book of Esther, the Lord's name is surprisingly not mentioned; however, it is clear that His counsel is at work in the hearts of His servants. When Queen Esther was made aware of the impending destruction that threatened her people due to the vendetta of Haman, she made the decision to ask her husband King Ahasuerus for help (Esther 4:8). Because this bold action may have resulted in her own death since she had not been personally summoned by the king, she devised a plan for all of the Jews in Shushan to fast for her for three days. Ultimately, she was granted favor by the king and her people's lives were spared.

The fear of the Lord is the beginning of wisdom: a good understanding have all they that do His commandments...
Psalm 111:10

Critical Thinking Habits

VanderMey (2014) lists several habits to increase critical thinking skills, some of which can also be referenced in the Bible. For example, he suggests that being focused is one of these habits, and the Bible states that when our mind is focused on the Lord, He will keep us in perfect peace (Isaiah 26:3). Testing the evidence is another activity that VanderMey supports, and the Bible also instructs us to "test the spirits to see whether they are from God" (1 John 4:1, AMP). In order to make a good decision—whether it is based on worldly statistics or scriptural references—we should implement the foundation of critical thinking.

The story of Samson and Delilah found in the Book of Judges is an example of what can happen when we do not test the evidence before making a decision. Samson judged Israel for twenty years, so he should have been applying critical thinking skills during that entire time. However, when it came to women, he appeared to be emotionally weak even though he had supernatural physical strength. The Philistines, Israel's long-time enemy, bribed Delilah to find out where Samson's strength came from and how they could defeat him. She asked Samson to tell her where his strength came from so he could be overcome (Judges 16:6). It was evident that Delilah was setting him up and although he lied to her three times, he eventually revealed that he would become weak if his hair was cut. That poor decision not only led to his capture, but to both of his eyes being gouged out. The only positive outcome was that Samson was able to regain his strength when his hair started to grow back, so he prayed to the Lord to be able to push down the pillars of the building where he was imprisoned. He actually killed more Philistines upon his death than he did during his lifetime (Judges 16:30).

But examine everything carefully; hold fast to that which is good. 1 Thessalonians 5:21, NASB

Sharlyne Carla

Critical Thinking in Decision-Making

How can we make good decisions using critical thinking? According to Henley and Mooz (2012), "A good decision selects the alternative with the best chance of achieving the desired outcome given the information available at the time" (p. 17). In order to identify the most favorable alternative, critical thinking tools such as analysis, evaluation, and reasoning must be applied.

For a Believer, this process begins by finding the answer in the Bible; and John 5:39 clearly instructs us to "search the scriptures." Obviously, this particular course of action does not apply to every minor decision that has little or no impact on others (such as what to wear to a special event), nor to a major decision that has to be made quickly due to unforeseen circumstances (such as a medical emergency). Whenever appropriate, however, thoughtful consideration should be made before each decision, even when it doesn't seem convenient. Why? Because individual decisions can affect entire groups of people.

The Bible warns us in Exodus 34:7 that God can impose a father's sins on his descendants all the way down to the fourth generation. Eli the priest learned this lesson the hard way in the First Book of Samuel. His two sons Hophni and Phinehas were sinning against the Lord in the temple and had also caused the children of Israel to sin. Eli talked to them about their evil deeds but he did not stop them, so the Lord sent a prophet to tell him that all of his male descendants would die young and not be able to serve as priests.

**The naive believe anything, but the prudent give thought to their steps.
Proverbs 14:15, CEB**

Decision-Making Process

Henley and Mooz use the phrase "decision fitness" (2012, p. 22-23) to describe the different aspects of arriving at the best solution to a problem. It is imperative that Believers pray for guidance, as their decisions should be based on all of the laws, commands, and instructions given in the scriptures that are applicable to their current issue. An article titled "Biblical Decision Making Steps" listed strategies similar to Henley and Mooz. For example, the author states that obtaining counsel and acting on your decision are part of this ten-step process (Fairchild, 2016, February 17), which coincides to getting comparative information and implementing action as noted by Henley and Mooz. One major difference between these two lists is that Fairchild admonishes the Believer to "be ready to accept and obey God's answer" (2016,

February 17). Ultimately, the faith-based decision should be in line with the Lord's perfect will.

Jesus is the foremost example for the Believer to follow, and He also had to pray and obey God. Before His crucifixion, Jesus prayed at the Mount of Olives for the Father's will to be done even though He knew how painful and agonizing that plan was (Luke 22:42). Jesus is referred to as "the Lamb slain from the foundation of the world" (Revelation 13:8), which implies that He didn't have a choice to go to the cross. However, if that was the case, then why does Matthew 26:53 say that He could have asked God to send an army of angels to rescue Him? It appears as though Jesus made a conscious, deliberate decision to die for our sins.

And if it seem evil unto you to serve the Lord, choose you this day whom ye will serve... but as for me and my house, we will serve the Lord. Joshua 24:15

Benefits of Good Decisions

The benefits of making a good decision can be both tangible and intangible. For example, if you make an informed decision to invest in the right stocks and they increase in value, you may receive dividends or passive income. Furthermore, you may also lower your blood pressure and stress levels by knowing that your stocks are doing well. Since "good decisions have a much higher probability of good outcomes" (Henley and Mooz, 2012, p. 18), shouldn't we strive to follow the proper decision-making protocol?

For the Believer, acquiring the desires of our heart as mentioned in Psalm 37 is also a benefit of critical thinking. Peach lists this benefit as the culmination of his "7 Step Biblical Decision Making Process," as he advises Believers that "when it comes down to choosing between two good choices and God does not give any clear direction, then the final step indicates that you can choose the one you most desire" (2011, June 26).

Abraham at age 100 and his wife Sarah at age 90 were blessed with their son Isaac in the twenty-first chapter of the Book of Genesis. Isaac was the promised child of the covenant that the Lord had made with Abraham. In chapter twenty-two, however, God told Abraham to sacrifice his long-awaited son. Not knowing the final outcome of obeying this strange and unexpected request, Abraham confidently ascended the mountain in Moriah with Isaac, a knife, and some firewood because of his steadfast faith as described in Romans 4:19. With this single decision to obey—which thankfully did not result in the death of Isaac—Abraham received the benefit of God's trust in addition to the promise indicated in Genesis 22:17-18 that he would be blessed and have countless descendants who would be victorious over their enemies and enable all nations to be blessed as well.

If they obey and serve Him, they shall spend their days in prosperity, and their years in pleasures. Job 36:11

Decision-Making Outcomes

The well-known adage that hindsight is twenty/twenty holds true in certain circumstances and should always be utilized as a learning tool, because the final outcome of decision-making will have either a positive or negative effect. Melé (2010) suggests that "practical wisdom introduces ethics in decision making by considering both the end or goal pursued and the means to achieve such an end from the perspective of the human good" (p. 641). Believers definitely need to think carefully about the totality of a matter before making any rash, ill-informed judgments. Throughout the Bible, we can find countless stories of people who made certain life-changing (or even history-making) decisions which either resulted in joy and peace or created consequences of turmoil and despair both individually and collectively.

On the positive side, when Ruth decided to accompany her mother-in-law Naomi back to Bethlehem when the famine ended (Ruth 1:16), she met and married Boaz and gave birth to a son named Obed, who was the grandfather of David in the lineage of Jesus. And when a hopeless widow in Zarephath decided to use her last handful of flour to make a cake of bread for the prophet Elijah instead of saving it for herself and her son before they starved to death (1 Kings 17:15), the Lord caused her food to multiply and also brought her son back to life when he later became ill.

On the negative side, when Moses decided to hit the rock to bring forth water for the children of Israel in the desert although the Lord had told him to speak to it (Numbers 20:11), he was punished by being replaced by Joshua as the person who led them into the promised land. And when Saul decided to disobey God by sparing the king of the

Amalekites and the best of their possessions (1 Samuel 15:9), he lost his own position as king of Israel and the prophet Samuel was sent to anoint David as his replacement.

Many are the plans of the human heart, but it is the decision of the Lord that endures. Proverbs 19:21, NABRE

Decision-Making Experience

After nearly half a century of living, I have made several transformative decisions that were based on pure impulse—neither critical thinking nor biblical reference. My first major decision was to move from California to Rhode Island in 1994 to obtain a higher college degree, and that goal was accomplished. However, that decision was made in haste only to escape the inevitable experience of future earthquakes. I was blessed to have my daughter during that time, but we had to endure cold winters alone without any relatives nearby.

My second impactful decision to move to Florida in 2003 was solely economically driven, as the cost of living was much lower there than in Rhode Island. Consequently, two layoffs approximately four years apart caused me great financial stress. This journey around the country could have been done more efficiently and with less effort to resolve unexpected issues that arose if a sensible decision-making process was in place and at work.

One of the most important decisions that I have made thus far was deliberated via a complementary blend of critical thinking and my now twenty-year-old Bible: I submitted my resignation from corporate America just hours before the ball dropped in Times Square on January 1, 2015. I was already a part-time entrepreneur as I have been publishing and editing books since 2007 and writing resumes since 2008. I also had a registered fictitious name for my prayer ministry since 2006. I filed my Articles of Incorporation for Spirit of Excellence Writing & Editing Services, LLC in 2014 in preparation for the transition.

On the practical, logical side, I had to consider my financial situation. My car would be paid off shortly thereafter, so that was a heavy weight lifted off of my shoulders. Also, not having a job would give me the freedom to network more and make additional business connections. Besides the fact that being at this particular job was more stressful than being unemployed years prior, I would have the opportunity to make a greater income by editing more books and writing resumes on my own schedule as an independent contractor.

On the spiritual, divine side, I had to meditate on and have blind faith for the manifestation of scriptures such as: "But my God shall supply all your need according to his riches in glory by Christ Jesus" (Philippians 4:19), and "For the Lord thy God hath blessed thee in all the works of thy hand" (Deuteronomy 2:7). I had been wanting and waiting for several months, literally in tears, to leave my last job; so as soon as the Lord gave me a prophetic word, I chose an end date and never looked back. I received the revelation that it was time to shift to another level of peace and prosperity, I waited for instructions on how and when to move, and I acted upon the faith that already resided in me.

Although I was completely operating in my own permissive will for the first thirty years of my life, God's perfect will was steering the path to my destiny in the background. When I totally surrendered myself to His authority, I became responsible for consulting the Holy Spirit before making any crucial choices. And while obtaining my MBA degree in 2017 for which the Lord provided a full scholarship, I also discovered an array of business-based resources that could help sharpen my decision-making skills.

And we know that all things work together for good to them that love God, to them who are the called according to His purpose. Romans 8:28

Conclusion

How can a Believer benefit from employing secular critical thinking methods in tandem with scripture? Some of the habits, tools, and steps used for successful decision-making in the business arena are also found in the Bible, so we should not put God in a box and assume that He can only use one vehicle or group of people to assist us with life's daily struggles. Just as we can refer to and subscribe to other forms of multimedia outside of our local church in order to be spiritually fed, we can also learn how to make good decisions by utilizing wisdom, knowledge, and understanding that can be found outside of the Bible as long as it does not contradict the Truth or dilute our faith.

Wisdom is the principal thing; therefore get wisdom: and with all thy getting get understanding. Proverbs 4:7

Use this page to record important decisions you need to make and the applicable scriptures you can pray and meditate on to help guide you. I suggest that you search for specific words or phrases on www.BibleGateway.com.

_____
_____
_____
_____
_____
_____
_____
_____
_____
_____
_____
_____
_____
_____
_____
_____
_____
_____
_____
_____
_____

Bibliography

Fairchild, M. (2016, February 17). Biblical decision making steps.

Henley, J., Mooz, H. (2012). *Make up your mind: A decision making guide to thinking clearly and choosing wisely*. John Wiley & Sons P&T. VitalBook.

Melé, D. (2010). Practical wisdom in managerial decision making. *The Journal of Management Development*, 29(7), 637-645.

Paul, R., Scriven, M. (1987, Summer). Critical thinking as defined by the National Council for Excellence in Critical Thinking, 1987.

Peach, D. (2011, June 26). 7 step biblical decision making process.

VanderMey, R. (2014). *The college writer: A guide to thinking, writing, and researching, 5th Edition*. Cengage Learning. VitalBook.

About the Author

Sharlyne C. Thomas, writing as **Sharlyne Carla**, is a professional editor, inspirational speaker, and award-winning author who has published five other non-fiction books thus far. She holds an MBA in Management, a 2-15 Life & Health Insurance License, and a Woman & Minority Business Certification. As Managing Member of Spirit of Excellence Writing & Editing Services, LLC, Sharlyne has contributed articles to periodicals such as *IBA Success Magazine* and *Built to Prosper* while editing and proofreading various copy for a broad range of writers and organizations nationwide.

Sharlyne has been invited to speak and teach at a variety of community and ministry events, including Destined for Destiny Women's Institute and the Central Florida Mayors Prayer Breakfast. She has also judged four business/beauty pageants and has been a guest on several radio and TV shows such as WOKB 1680AM, Rejoice 1140AM, *Point of View* on the Afrotainment Channel, and *Atlanta Live* on WATC-TV 57.

In addition to serving as an Ambassador with the African American Chamber of Commerce of Central Florida and a Member of Women on the Rise Orlando, Sharlyne is the Founder of Sword of the Spirit Ministries Florida, Inc., a 501c3 nonprofit charity organization created to empower single parents and their children to become more productive citizens spiritually, physically, and financially. Born and raised in Southern California, she currently lives in Central Florida.

Contact Information

Sharlyne Carla, Kingdom Ambassador
www.facebook.com/takeupthysword
sharlynecarla@gmail.com
321-209-2309

Please feel free to contact the author with any questions, comments, or prayer requests. She is available for book club presentations, signings, and speaking engagements for your business or church, including special events, workshops, conferences, retreats, and seminars. Other works by the author can be purchased at www.TakeUpThySword.com: